APOSTOLIC CONS

ANGLICANORUM COETIBUS

BENEDICT XVI

PROVIDING FOR PERSONAL ORDINARIATES
FOR ANGLICANS ENTERING INTO FULL
COMMUNION WITH THE CATHOLIC CHURCH

*All booklets are published thanks to the generous support
of the members of the Catholic Truth Society*

CATHOLIC TRUTH SOCIETY
PUBLISHERS TO THE HOLY SEE

Contents

APOSTOLIC CONSTITUTION

ANGLICANORUM COETIBUS

In recent times the Holy Spirit has moved groups of Anglicans to petition repeatedly and insistently to be received into full Catholic communion individually as well as corporately. The Apostolic See has responded favourably to such petitions. Indeed, the successor of Peter, mandated by the Lord Jesus to guarantee the unity of the episcopate and to preside over and safeguard the universal communion of all the Churches,[1] could not fail to make available the means necessary to bring this holy desire to realisation.

The Church, a people gathered into the unity of the Father, the Son and the Holy Spirit,[2] was instituted by our Lord Jesus Christ, as "a sacrament – a sign and instrument, that is, of communion with God and of unity among all people."[3] Every division among the baptised in Jesus Christ wounds that which the Church is and that for which the Church exists; in fact, "such division openly contradicts the will of Christ, scandalizes the world, and damages that most holy cause of preaching the Gospel to every creature."[4] Precisely

---

[1] Cf. Second Vatican Council, Dogmatic Constitution *Lumen gentium*, 23; Congregation for the Doctrine of the Faith, Letter *Communionis notio*, 12; 13.

[2] Cf. Dogmatic Constitution *Lumen gentium*, 4; Decree *Unitatis redintegratio*, 2.

[3] Dogmatic Constitution *Lumen gentium*, 1.

[4] Decree *Unitatis redintegratio*, 1.

for this reason, before shedding his blood for the salvation of the world, the Lord Jesus prayed to the Father for the unity of his disciples.[5]

It is the Holy Spirit, the principle of unity, which establishes the Church as a communion.[6] He is the principle of the unity of the faithful in the teaching of the Apostles, in the breaking of the bread and in prayer.[7] The Church, however, analogous to the mystery of the Incarnate Word, is not only an invisible spiritual communion, but is also visible;[8] in fact, "the society structured with hierarchical organs and the Mystical Body of Christ, the visible society and the spiritual community, the earthly Church and the Church endowed with heavenly riches, are not to be thought of as two realities. On the contrary, they form one complex reality formed from a two-fold element, human and divine."[9] The communion of the baptised in the teaching of the Apostles and in the breaking of the eucharistic bread is visibly manifested in the bonds of the profession of the faith in its entirety, of the celebration of all of the sacraments instituted by Christ, and of the governance of the College of Bishops united with its head, the Roman Pontiff.[10]

This single Church of Christ, which we profess in the Creed as one, holy, catholic and apostolic "subsists in the Catholic Church, which is governed by the successor of Peter and by

---

[5] Cf. *Jn* 17:20-21; Decree *Unitatis redintegratio*, 2.

[6] Cf. Dogmatic Constitution *Lumen gentium*, 13.

[7] Cf. *ibid*; *Ac* 2:42.

[8] Cf. Dogmatic Constitution *Lumen gentium*, 8; Letter *Communionis notio*, 4.

[9] Dogmatic Constitution *Lumen gentium*, 8.

[10] Cf. CIC, can. 205; Dogmatic Constitution *Lumen gentium*, 13; 14; 21; 22; Decree *Unitatis redintegratio*, 2; 3; 4; 15; 20; Decree *Christus Dominus*, 4; Decree *Ad gentes*, 22.

the Bishops in communion with him. Nevertheless, many elements of sanctification and of truth are found outside her visible confines. Since these are gifts properly belonging to the Church of Christ, they are forces impelling towards Catholic unity."[11]

In the light of these ecclesiological principles, this Apostolic Constitution provides the general normative structure for regulating the institution and life of Personal Ordinariates for those Anglican faithful who desire to enter into the full communion of the Catholic Church in a corporate manner. This Constitution is completed by Complementary Norms issued by the Apostolic See.

I. §1 Personal Ordinariates for Anglicans entering into full communion with the Catholic Church are erected by the Congregation for the Doctrine of the Faith within the confines of the territorial boundaries of a particular Conference of Bishops in consultation with that same Conference.

§2 Within the territory of a particular Conference of Bishops, one or more Ordinariates may be erected as needed.

§3 Each Ordinariate possesses public juridic personality by the law itself (*ipso iure*); it is juridically comparable to a diocese.[12]

---

[11] Dogmatic Constitution *Lumen gentium*, 8.
[12] Cf. John Paul II, Ap. Const. *Spirituali militium curae*, 21st April 1986, I § 1.

§4 The Ordinariate is composed of lay faithful, clerics and members of Institutes of Consecrated Life and Societies of Apostolic Life, originally belonging to the Anglican Communion and now in full communion with the Catholic Church, or those who receive the Sacraments of Initiation within the jurisdiction of the Ordinariate.

§5 The *Catechism of the Catholic Church* is the authoritative expression of the Catholic faith professed by members of the Ordinariate.

II. The Personal Ordinariate is governed according to the norms of universal law and the present Apostolic Constitution and is subject to the Congregation for the Doctrine of the Faith, and the other Dicasteries of the Roman Curia in accordance with their competencies. It is also governed by the Complementary Norms as well as any other specific Norms given for each Ordinariate.

III. Without excluding liturgical celebrations according to the Roman Rite, the Ordinariate has the faculty to celebrate the Holy Eucharist and the other Sacraments, the Liturgy of the Hours and other liturgical celebrations according to the liturgical books proper to the Anglican tradition, which have been approved by the Holy See, so as to maintain the liturgical, spiritual and pastoral traditions of the Anglican Communion within the Catholic Church, as a precious gift nourishing the faith of the members of the Ordinariate and as a treasure to be shared.

IV. A Personal Ordinariate is entrusted to the pastoral care of an Ordinary appointed by the Roman Pontiff.

V. The power (*potestas*) of the Ordinary is:

a. *ordinary*: connected by the law itself to the office entrusted to him by the Roman Pontiff, for both the internal forum and external forum;

b. *vicarious*: exercised in the name of the Roman Pontiff;

c. *personal*: exercised over all who belong to the Ordinariate.

This power is *to be exercised jointly* with that of the local Diocesan Bishop, in those cases provided for in the Complementary Norms.

VI. § 1. Those who ministered as Anglican deacons, priests, or bishops, and who fulfill the requisites established by canon law[13] and are not impeded by irregularities or other impediments[14] may be accepted by the Ordinary as candidates for Holy Orders in the Catholic Church. In the case of married ministers, the norms established in the Encyclical Letter of Pope Paul VI *Sacerdotalis coelibatus*, n. 42[15] and in the Statement *In June*[16] are to be observed. Unmarried ministers must submit to the norm of clerical celibacy of CIC can. 277, §1.

---

[13] Cf. *CIC*, cann. 1026-1032.
[14] Cf. *CIC*, cann. 1040-1049.
[15] Cf. *AAS* 59 (1967) 674.
[16] Cf. Congregation for the Doctrine of the Faith, *Statement of 1st April 1981*, in *Enchiridion Vaticanum* 7, 1213.

§ 2. The Ordinary, in full observance of the discipline of celibate clergy in the Latin Church, as a rule (*pro regula*) will admit only celibate men to the order of presbyter. He may also petition the Roman Pontiff, as a derogation from can. 277, §1, for the admission of married men to the order of presbyter on a case by case basis, according to objective criteria approved by the Holy See.

§ 3. Incardination of clerics will be regulated according to the norms of canon law.

§ 4. Priests incardinated into an Ordinariate, who constitute the presbyterate of the Ordinariate, are also to cultivate bonds of unity with the presbyterate of the Diocese in which they exercise their ministry. They should promote common pastoral and charitable initiatives and activities, which can be the object of agreements between the Ordinary and the local Diocesan Bishop.

§ 5. Candidates for Holy Orders in an Ordinariate should be prepared alongside other seminarians, especially in the areas of doctrinal and pastoral formation. In order to address the particular needs of seminarians of the Ordinariate and formation in Anglican patrimony, the Ordinary may also establish seminary programs or houses of formation which would relate to existing Catholic faculties of theology.

VII. The Ordinary, with the approval of the Holy See, can erect new Institutes of Consecrated Life and Societies of Apostolic Life, with the right to call their members to Holy

Orders, according to the norms of canon law. Institutes of Consecrated Life originating in the Anglican Communion and entering into full communion with the Catholic Church may also be placed under his jurisdiction by mutual consent.

VIII. § 1. The Ordinary, according to the norm of law, after having heard the opinion of the Diocesan Bishop of the place, may erect, with the consent of the Holy See, personal parishes for the faithful who belong to the Ordinariate.

§ 2. Pastors of the Ordinariate enjoy all the rights and are held to all the obligations established in the Code of Canon Law and, in cases established by the Complementary Norms, such rights and obligations are to be exercised in mutual pastoral assistance together with the pastors of the local Diocese where the personal parish of the Ordinariate has been established.

IX. Both the lay faithful as well as members of Institutes of Consecrated Life and Societies of Apostolic Life, originally part of the Anglican Communion, who wish to enter the Personal Ordinariate, must manifest this desire in writing.

X.§ 1. The Ordinary is aided in his governance by a Governing Council with its own statutes approved by the Ordinary and confirmed by the Holy See.[17]

§ 2. The Governing Council, presided over by the Ordinary, is composed of at least six priests. It exercises the functions

---

[17] Cf. *CIC*, cann. 495-502.

specified in the Code of Canon Law for the Presbyteral Council and the College of Consultors, as well as those areas specified in the Complementary Norms.

§ 3. The Ordinary is to establish a Finance Council according to the norms established by the Code of Canon Law which will exercise the duties specified therein.[18]

§ 4. In order to provide for the consultation of the faithful, a Pastoral Council is to be constituted in the Ordinariate.[19]

XI. Every five years the Ordinary is required to come to Rome for an *ad limina Apostolorum* visit and present to the Roman Pontiff, through the Congregation for the Doctrine of the Faith and in consultation with the Congregation for Bishops and the Congregation for the Evangelisation of Peoples, a report on the status of the Ordinariate.

XII. For judicial cases, the competent tribunal is that of the Diocese in which one of the parties is domiciled, unless the Ordinariate has constituted its own tribunal, in which case the tribunal of second instance is the one designated by the Ordinariate and approved by the Holy See.

XIII. The Decree establishing an Ordinariate will determine the location of the See and, if appropriate, the principal church.

---

[18] Cf. *CIC*, cann. 492-494.
[19] Cf. *CIC*, can. 511.

12

We desire that our dispositions and norms be valid and effective now and in the future, notwithstanding, should it be necessary, the Apostolic Constitutions and ordinances issued by our predecessors, or any other prescriptions, even those requiring special mention or derogation.

Given in Rome, at St Peter's, on 4th November 2009, the Memorial of St Charles Borromeo.

BENEDICTUS PP. XVI

COMPLEMENTARY NORMS
FOR THE APOSTOLIC CONSTITUTION

ANGLICANORUM COETIBUS

Jurisdiction of the Holy See

Article 1

Each Ordinariate is subject to the *Congregation for the Doctrine of the Faith*. It maintains close relations with the other Roman Dicasteries in accordance with their competence.

Relations with Episcopal Conferences and Diocesan Bishops

Article 2

§1. The Ordinary follows the directives of the national Episcopal Conference insofar as this is consistent with the norms contained in the Apostolic Constitution *Anglicanorum coetibus*.

§2. The Ordinary is a member of the respective Episcopal Conference.

Article 3

The Ordinary, in the exercise of this office, must maintain close ties of communion with the Bishop of the Diocese in which the Ordinariate is present in order to coordinate its pastoral activity with the pastoral program of the Diocese.

The Ordinary

Article 4

§1. The Ordinary may be a bishop or a presbyter appointed by the Roman Pontiff *ad nutum Sanctae Sedis*, based on a terna presented by the Governing Council. Canons 383-388, 392-394, and 396-398 of the Code of Canon Law apply to him.

§2. The Ordinary has the faculty to incardinate in the Ordinariate former Anglican ministers who have entered into full communion with the Catholic Church, as well as candidates belonging to the Ordinariate and promoted to Holy Orders by him.

§3. Having first consulted with the Episcopal Conference and obtained the consent of the Governing Council and the approval of the Holy See, the Ordinary can erect as needed territorial deaneries supervised by a delegate of the Ordinary covering the faithful of multiple personal parishes.

The Faithful of the Ordinariate

Article 5

§1. The lay faithful originally of the Anglican tradition who wish to belong to the Ordinariate, after having made their Profession of Faith and received the Sacraments of Initiation, with due regard for Canon 845, are to be entered in the apposite register of the Ordinariate. Those baptised previously as Catholics outside the Ordinariate are not ordinarily eligible for membership, unless they are members of a family belonging to the Ordinariate.

§2. Lay faithful and members of Institutes of Consecrated Life and Societies of Apostolic Life, when they collaborate in pastoral or charitable activities, whether diocesan or parochial, are subject to the Diocesan Bishop or to the pastor of the place; in which case the power of the Diocesan Bishop or pastor is exercised jointly with that of the Ordinary and the pastor of the Ordinariate.

The Clergy

Article 6

§1. In order to admit candidates to Holy Orders the Ordinary must obtain the consent of the Governing Council. In consideration of Anglican ecclesial tradition and practice, the Ordinary may present to the Holy Father a request for the admission of married men to the presbyterate in the Ordinariate, after a process of discernment based on

17

objective criteria and the needs of the Ordinariate. These objective criteria are determined by the Ordinary in consultation with the local Episcopal Conference and must be approved by the Holy See.

§2. Those who have been previously ordained in the Catholic Church and subsequently have become Anglicans, may not exercise sacred ministry in the Ordinariate. Anglican clergy who are in irregular marriage situations may not be accepted for Holy Orders in the Ordinariate.

§3. Presbyters incardinated in the Ordinariate receive the necessary faculties from the Ordinary.

Article 7

§1 The Ordinary must ensure that adequate remuneration be provided to the clergy incardinated in the Ordinariate, and must provide for their needs in the event of sickness, disability, and old age.

§2. The Ordinary will enter into discussion with the Episcopal Conference about resources and funds which might be made available for the care of the clergy of the Ordinariate.

§3. When necessary, priests, with the permission of the Ordinary, may engage in a secular profession compatible with the exercise of priestly ministry (cf. *CIC*, can. 286).

Article 8

§1. The presbyters, while constituting the presbyterate of the Ordinariate, are eligible for membership in the Presbyteral Council of the Diocese in which they exercise pastoral care of the faithful of the Ordinariate (cf. *CIC*, can. 498, §2).

§2. Priests and Deacons incardinated in the Ordinariate may be members of the Pastoral Council of the Diocese in which they exercise their ministry, in accordance with the manner determined by the Diocesan Bishop (cf. *CIC*, can. 512, §1).

Article 9

§1. The clerics incardinated in the Ordinariate should be available to assist the Diocese in which they have a domicile or quasi-domicile, where it is deemed suitable for the pastoral care of the faithful. In such cases they are subject to the Diocesan Bishop in respect to that which pertains to the pastoral charge or office they receive.

§2. Where and when it is deemed suitable, clergy incardinated in a Diocese or in an Institute of Consecrated Life or a Society of Apostolic Life, with the written consent of their respective Diocesan Bishop or their Superior, can collaborate in the pastoral care of the Ordinariate. In such case they are subject to the Ordinary in respect to that which pertains to the pastoral charge or office they receive.

§3. In the cases treated in the preceding paragraphs there should be a written agreement between the Ordinary and the Diocesan Bishop or the Superior of the Institute of Consecrated Life or the Moderator of the Society of Apostolic Life, in which the terms of collaboration and all that pertains to the means of support are clearly established.

Article 10

§1. Formation of the clergy of the Ordinariate should accomplish two objectives:

1) joint formation with diocesan seminarians in accordance with local circumstances;

2) formation, in full harmony with Catholic tradition, in those aspects of the Anglican patrimony that are of particular value.

§2. Candidates for priestly ordination will receive their theological formation with other seminarians at a seminary or a theological faculty in conformity with an agreement concluded between the Ordinary and, respectively, the Diocesan Bishop or Bishops concerned. Candidates may receive other aspects of priestly formation at a seminary program or house of formation established, with the consent of the Governing Council, expressly for the purpose of transmitting Anglican patrimony.

§3. The Ordinariate must have its own Program of Priestly Formation, approved by the Holy See; each house of formation should draw up its own rule, approved by the Ordinary (cf. *CIC*, can. 242, §1).

§4. The Ordinary may accept as seminarians only those faithful who belong to a personal parish of the Ordinariate or who were previously Anglican and have established full communion with the Catholic Church.

§5. The Ordinariate sees to the continuing formation of its clergy, through their participation in local programs provided by the Episcopal Conference and the Diocesan Bishop.

Former Anglican Bishops

Article 11

§1. A married former Anglican Bishop is eligible to be appointed Ordinary. In such a case he is to be ordained a priest in the Catholic Church and then exercises pastoral and sacramental ministry within the Ordinariate with full jurisdictional authority.

§2. A former Anglican Bishop who belongs to the Ordinariate may be called upon to assist the Ordinary in the administration of the Ordinariate.

§3. A former Anglican Bishop who belongs to the Ordinariate may be invited to participate in the meetings of the Bishops' Conference of the respective territory, with the equivalent status of a retired bishop.

§4. A former Anglican Bishop who belongs to the Ordinariate and who has not been ordained as a bishop in the Catholic Church, may request permission from the Holy See to use the insignia of the episcopal office.

The Governing Council

Article 12

§1. The Governing Council, in accord with Statutes which the Ordinary must approve, will have the rights and responsibilities accorded by the *Code of Canon Law* to the College of Consultors and the Presbyteral Council.

§2. In addition to these responsibilities, the Ordinary needs the consent of the Governing Council to:

a. admit a candidate to Holy Orders;

b. erect or suppress a personal parish;

c. erect or suppress a house of formation;

d. approve a program of formation.

§3. The Ordinary also consults the Governing Council

a. concerning the pastoral activities of the Ordinariate and the principles governing the formation of clergy.

§4. The Governing Council has a deliberative vote:

a. when choosing a *terna* of names to submit to the Holy See for the appointment of the Ordinary;

b. when proposing changes to the Complementary Norms of the Ordinariate to present to the Holy See;

c. when formulating the Statutes of the Governing

Council, the Statutes of the Pastoral Council, and the Rule for houses of formation.

§ 5. The Governing Council is composed according to the Statutes of the Council. Half of the membership is elected by the priests of the Ordinariate.

The Pastoral Council

Article 13

§1. The Pastoral Council, constituted by the Ordinary, offers advice regarding the pastoral activity of the Ordinariate.

§2. The Pastoral Council, whose president is the Ordinary, is governed by Statutes approved by the Ordinary.

The Personal Parishes

Article 14

§1. The pastor may be assisted in the pastoral care of the parish by a parochial vicar, appointed by the Ordinary; a pastoral council and a finance council must be established in the parish.

§2. If there is no vicar, in the event of absence, incapacity, or death of the pastor, the pastor of the territorial parish in which the church of the personal parish is located can exercise his faculties as pastor so as to supply what is needed.

§3. For the pastoral care of the faithful who live within the boundaries of a Diocese in which no personal parish has been erected, the Ordinary, having heard the opinion of the local Diocesan Bishop, can make provisions for quasi-parishes (cf. *CIC*, can. 516, §1).

The Supreme Pontiff Benedict XVI, at the Audience granted to the undersigned Cardinal Prefect, approved these Complementary Norms for the Apostolic Constitution **Anglicanorum coetibus***, adopted in the Ordinary Session of the Congregation, and ordered their publication.*

Rome, from the Offices of the Congregation for the Doctrine of the Faith, 4th November 2009, the Memorial of St Charles Borromeo.

William Card. Levada
Prefect

Luis. F. Ladaria, S.J.
Titular Archbishop of Thibica
Secretary